For Ebony

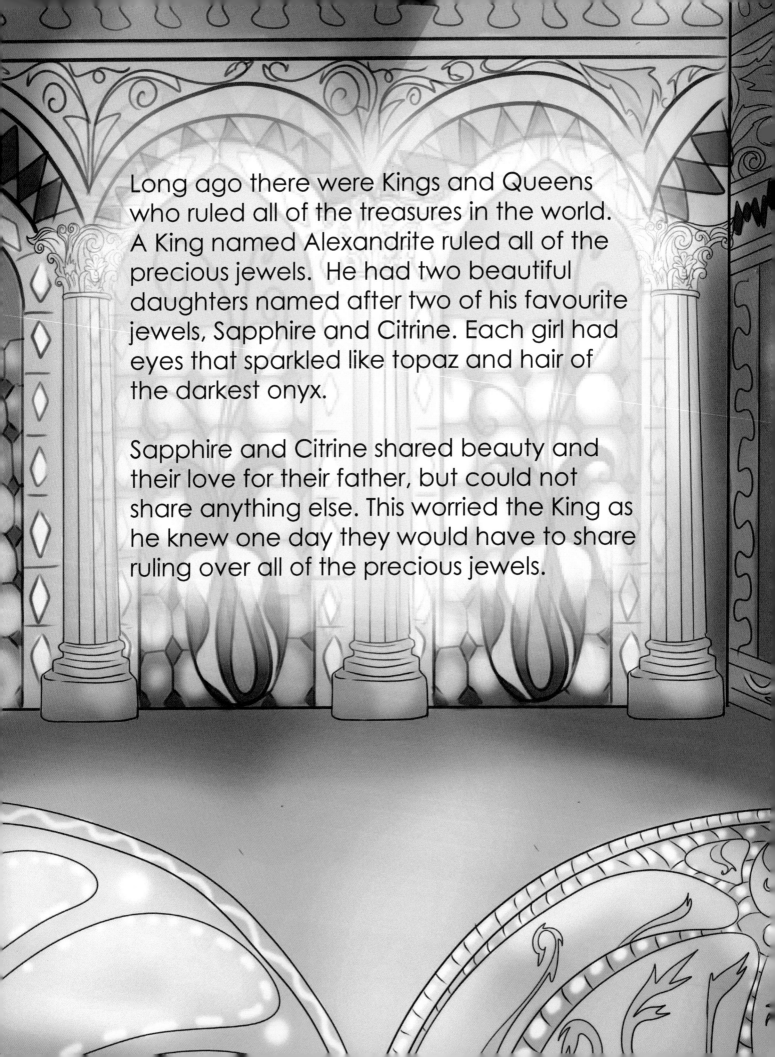

Long ago there were Kings and Queens who ruled all of the treasures in the world. A King named Alexandrite ruled all of the precious jewels. He had two beautiful daughters named after two of his favourite jewels, Sapphire and Citrine. Each girl had eyes that sparkled like topaz and hair of the darkest onyx.

Sapphire and Citrine shared beauty and their love for their father, but could not share anything else. This worried the King as he knew one day they would have to share ruling over all of the precious jewels.

After watching his daughters argue one day, King Alexandrite turned to Mother Nature in despair. "Dearest Mother Nature what shall I do? My daughters are so alike yet quarrel like I have never known." Mother Nature gazed upon Alexandrite with her kind eyes "If the girls learn to give away all they have they will have more than ever, including their sister's love" she replied.

The sun shone high in the sky the following morning and the girls played by the sea shore. King Alexandrite gathered his smoothest coral. He laid the beautiful stones before the girls, varying in every shade. Sapphire and Citrine began looking at each stone carefully, making piles of their favourite pieces.

Sadly the girls grew jealous of the stones the other had. Before King Alexandrite knew it, the girls were snatching pieces from each other. Back and forth the coral went until there was a great - splash!

They could only watch as the coral was tossed into the sea, making wonderful shapes as it reached the bottom.

Once the pieces settled, Sapphire and Citrine saw that the coral had made homes for all of the little fish who lived at the bottom of the sea. King Alexandrite watched as the girls smiled at the fish as they swam to and fro amongst the coral. But the girls frowned at each other. He knew that he would have to try again.

The moon hung low that night in an almost empty sky. King Alexandrite showed his girls a small cloth bag. Inside was a cluster of diamonds that twinkled as they reflected the light of the moon.

Sapphire and Citrine both grabbed at the small cloth bag. Back and forth it went until – whoosh.

They could only watch as every tiny diamond flew into the air. Sapphire and Citrine waited with their arms open wide to catch the diamonds as they fell back to earth. But the diamonds hung in the sky. The night sky shone

brighter than ever as the diamonds sparkled for all to see. King Alexandrite watched as the girls smiled at each and every diamond in the sky, but frowned at each other. He knew that he would have to try again.

King Alexandrite loved when his girls smiled.
"If there is only one thing they will have to share." he thought to himself. He searched for his shiniest emerald he could find and a ball of the softest velvet. Threading the emeralds onto the velvet, he made a beautiful necklace.

The King asked each girl to each hold out one hand.
Standing side by side the two girls held out a hand.
King Alexandrite hung the emerald necklace from
both of the girls' hands. Sapphire and Citrine's hands
clenched into fists around the emeralds. They yanked
the necklace back and forth until – ping!

The soft velvet snapped and the emerald
tumbled to the ground. They bounced off
the hard floors and immediately sank into the
soil. The emeralds resurfaced as green shoots
presenting pods. Sapphire and Citrine watched
as mice and other little creatures began
climbing the shoots and dining on the shiny
green peas inside the pods.
King Alexandrite watched as the girls smiled as
the creatures dined on the peas, but frowned at
each other. He knew that he would have to try
again.

Disappointed with his daughter's short lived happiness, King Alexandrite turned again to Mother Nature.
"Dearest Mother Nature what do I do? My daughters only want for themselves."

Mother Nature took a jewel from his robe made of hematite. She gently blew on the jewel and watched as it uncoiled into a caterpillar.

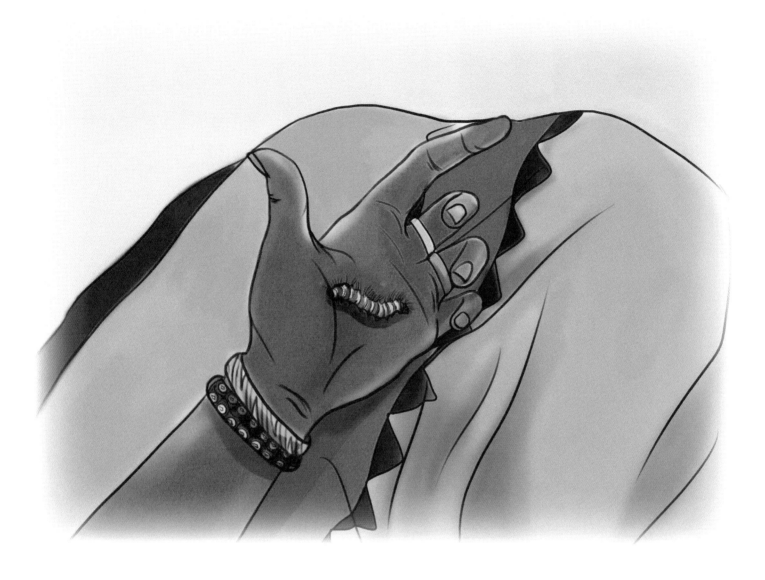

"This may help." she said as she carefully placed it on the palm of his hand.

King Alexandrite asked his daughters to sit by the peas to present them with their final gift. On a leaf, he placed the caterpillar. He watched as both girls sneered at the little creature. However, Sapphire and Citrine couldn't help but watch as Its little body stretched and squashed as it travelled along the plant.

"Take care of him" the King said "He's a precious jewel too".

Sapphire and Citrine watched for days as the little caterpillar travelled around the peas in the garden. The King was so pleased that he had found something the girls were able to share.

One morning King Alexandrite was awoken by shrieks as Sapphire and Citrine found that their hematite caterpillar was gone. In its place was a delicate paper like bag that hung from one of the pea pods.

Together, they made a bed of leaves and flowers for
their little caterpillar. They waited and waited and
waited.

They had almost given up hope when one day, the little paper like bag tore. Out climbed a beautiful, elegant butterfly.

Sapphire and Citrine danced and hugged each other for the very first time. Their butterfly flew into the air to join a kaleidoscope of butterflies that swirled in the sky.

Pleased that the girls had finally found their love for one another, Mother Nature decided to make Sapphire and Citrine the butterfly princesses. They were responsible for ensuring all the butterflies were always cared for.

The hematite butterfly returns every year to find the sweet emerald peas in Sapphire and Citrine's garden. He brings all of the other butterflies, knowing that the girls will share them all.